The Student's
TOOLBOX

TIPS FOR BETTER PLANNING

ANGELA ROYSTON

Gareth Stevens
Publishing

Please visit our website, www.garethstevens.com. For a free color catalog of all our
high-quality books, call toll free 1-800-542-2595 or fax 1-877-542-2596.

Library of Congress Cataloging-in-Publication Data

Royston, Angela, 1945-
Tips for better planning / Angela Royston.
    pages cm. — (The student's toolbox)
Includes index.
ISBN 978-1-4824-0172-1 (pbk.)
ISBN 978-1-4824-0173-8 (6-pack)
ISBN 978-1-4824-0167-7 (library binding)
1. Educational planning. 2. Social planning. 3. Students—Life skills guides. I. Title.
LB2806.R69 2014
371.2'07—dc23

2013028174

First Edition

Published in 2014 by
Gareth Stevens Publishing
111 East 14th Street, Suite 349
New York, NY 10003

© 2014 Gareth Stevens Publishing

Produced by Calcium, www.calciumcreative.co.uk
Designed by Emma Debanks and Paul Myerscough
Edited by Sarah Eason and Ronne Randall

Photo credits: Cover: Shutterstock: Mandy Godbehear. Inside: Dreamstime: Dianepix 19, Sonya
Etchison 13; Shutterstock: Africa Studio 6, Anneka 5, Bikeriderlondon 26, CandyBox Images 4,
Dotshock 11, Goodluz 27, Gow27 22, Darrin Henry 10, Paul Michael Hughes 23, Denis Kuvaev
9, Littleny 29, Lucky Business 1, 15, Markus Mainka 17, Rob Marmion 21, Monkey Business
Images 7, 24, Nattika 14, Oliveromg 28, Patrimonio Designs Ltd 25, Szefei 16, Videnko 12,
You Touch Pix of EuToch 8, Lisa F. Young 20, Cristian Zamfir 18.

Printed in the United States of America

CPSIA compliance information: Batch #CW14GS: For further information contact Gareth Stevens, New York, New York at 1-800-542-2595.

CONTENTS

WHY PLAN?

Are there lots of things you want to do next weekend? Do you need to buy your friend a birthday present? Whatever you are doing, it will go more smoothly if you plan it first. If you wander from one thing to another, you will forget some things, be late for others, and not get everything done. Planning saves time and puts you in control.

What's the Point?

Before making a plan, decide what your objective is. What is it you want to achieve? This might sound obvious, but focusing on the outcome helps you think clearly about what you have to do. You can then plan how to achieve the task more effectively.

You might say your objective is to do your homework, but maybe your real objective is to do your homework before watching a big game on television. If so, you need to build that into your planning!

Don't waste time by daydreaming or being distracted by your friends!

Keep an eye on how long you are taking to carry out each part of your plan.

PLAN YOUR TIME

TIPS FOR SUCCESS

You know what you want to do, but can you do it in time? Here are some tips to help you:

- **Make a list:** Write down all of the things you have to do.
- **Estimate:** How long do you think it will take to do each thing? Add the times together.
- **Allocate time:** When do you have to finish everything by? Do you have enough time, or will you have to do some things more quickly? Try to accurately assess how long each task will take you.

MAKING A PLAN

Every plan begins with a list! Write down all the things you have to do. Now you have to decide the order in which to do them. Should you do the most important thing first, or should you do the quickest thing first? Do you have to do one thing before you can do another? Does something have to be done by a particular time?

Routine or Recipe?

There isn't one simple rule to decide what to do first. If you do something regularly, such as getting ready for bed, you probably follow a routine. You don't have to think about what comes first. However, doing something complicated is different.

People often follow a recipe when they are cooking. The recipe tells them what they need, what to do, and what order to do it in. A cookbook recipe is a good model for making a plan.

A recipe tells you what to do and in what order.

> *If you are cooking or eating, add "clean up" to your plan!*

Everyday Tasks

It might sound boring, but planning everyday tasks such as doing the dishes or cleaning your bedroom become far simpler if you plan how much time they will take and when you are going to do them.

CHECK IT OFF!

Once you've decided the order in which to do things, a checklist will make sure you stay on track:

Check it off: Cross out each thing on your list when you've done it.

Make progress: Checking things off will give you a sense of progress as you see your list getting shorter!

Keep on target: Check how much you still have to do and figure out how much time you need to complete it.

IS THE PLAN WORKING?

Your plan may work perfectly, but what happens if it goes wrong? Suppose you've planned a picnic and it rains that day, or something takes much longer to do than you expected. Then you might have to change or adjust your plan. The important thing is to always keep your objective in mind.

Changing the Plan

Think ahead about what might go wrong with your plan. You might want to finish a list of chores in the morning, but suppose you run out of time. Which of the chores could be done later instead? You've decided to buy a particular DVD as a present for someone, but suppose it is sold out. What can you buy as a present instead?

Sometimes you have to have an alternative plan—plan B—in case things go wrong. If it rains on your picnic, for example, could you have the party at home instead?

If you are planning to do something outdoors, always check the weather forecast ahead of time.

Stay focused on what you are doing—don't get distracted by other people!

AVOIDING PROBLEMS

Some problems are unavoidable and you have to change your plans. However, other hazards can be avoided. Here are some tips for keeping your plan on track:

- **Start on time:** Make sure you don't start late.
- **Stay focused:** Don't get sidetracked into doing something else.
- **Keep checking:** Make sure your plan is working and, if not, be prepared to adjust it.
- **Don't get stuck on one thing:** If something is more difficult than you expected, get help with it or leave it until later.

READY FOR SCHOOL?

Are you always rushing to get to school on time? Do you rely on someone else to get you up and going, and out of the door? Now is the time to take control! Being in charge of yourself in the morning is good practice for getting to places on time when you are older.

Saving Time

Figure out how long it actually takes you to get up and ready for school. For example, how long does it take to get dressed in the morning? How long do you need to eat breakfast and to pack your schoolbag? How long do you normally take to brush your teeth? Set an alarm clock to wake you up in good time. That way you'll make sure that you start the day early enough to get everything done on time.

Good planning means being sensible. Don't overfill your schoolbag—take only what you really need!

Don't forget to take extra things you need on particular days. If you have a swimming lesson, remember to pack your swimming things.

The Night Before

Save time by getting as much as possible ready the night before. For example, decide which clothes you are going to wear and have them ready. Each night, check what activities you have for the next day, so you can pack your bag for the following day. That way you will have less to do in the morning. You may even be able to grab a few more minutes in bed!

PLANNING AHEAD

TIPS FOR SUCCESS

Make a checklist of the things you need to take to school. Before you go to bed, check that everything is ready for the next day:

- Have you done all your homework?
- Have you packed your schoolbag?
- Have you got the clothes you need for sports or other activities?
- Do you need to take a musical instrument?
- Do you need money?

PLAN YOUR DAY

On the weekends and during school vacations, you can relax—or can you? You may have lots of things arranged and other things you want to do, too. Can you fit them all in and still have time to relax? Relaxing is important. It gives your mind time to recharge, a little like a battery. However, you don't want to get bored. What you need is a balance!

School Days

While you are at school, your day is mostly planned for you. You don't have to think about what to do next. When school is over, though, you may have different possibilities. Do you have after-school activities that you do on particular days?

What do you do when you get home? You need to plan when you are going to relax and when you will do homework or music practice. By planning you will ensure that you find time to get things done, and relax, too.

Make sure you take some time out to enjoy yourself.

Planning to have fun with friends or to do a sport or hobby is as important as planning to do tasks such as homework.

MAKE A TIMETABLE

Whether you are planning what to do for a day, a whole weekend, or an evening, use these tips to help you make the most of your time:

- Do you have to do something at a fixed time? If so, allow extra time to meet the deadline.
- Decide what you can fit in before and after the fixed-time events.
- Don't try to fit in too much. You could end up rushing around and not enjoying anything.
- Include time to chill!

CHAPTER THREE

PLANNING FOR SCHOOL

How much time do you spend on homework in the evening? As you get older and move on to high school and college, you will be expected to do more work at home on your own. It's a good idea to get used to planning this now, so you get used to it and it becomes a normal routine.

The Best Strategy

If possible, always try to do your homework in the same place and at the same time every night. Then it will become a routine. Choose a quiet place where you will not be interrupted or distracted. You will be able to complete your homework more quickly and on time if you focus on it quietly.

Get everything you need together before you start your homework.

Prioritize Your Workload

If you have more than one thing to do for homework, decide in which order you will do them. Most people advise that you should do the most difficult piece of work first, before your brain becomes tired, so you can really focus on the task. You can do less difficult tasks, that are still manageable even if you are tired, later.

If you often find your homework too difficult, ask your teacher for some help.

MANAGING TIME

TIPS FOR SUCCESS

To find out how long you should be taking to do homework, multiply your grade by 10. For example, you should be spending 40 minutes in grade 4, and 50 minutes in grade 5. If you are taking longer than this, ask your teacher how long you should take. You might be doing more than you need to. Here are some tips for working faster:

- **Think first:** First figure out what you are going to do.
- **Stay focused:** Concentrate on what you are doing.
- **Take breaks:** If you get tired, take a short break and have a healthy snack before you continue.

PLANNING A PROJECT

How do you plan a big project, such as a project for school? There are so many things to do and so many things to remember! The answer is to split a big project up into several stages. For example, a project for school might consist of three main stages—research, writing, and presentation.

From Research to Presentation

Plan each stage of a project separately. Make a timetable to show what you have to do by when. This will help you finish everything on time. When planning research, make a list of what you need to find out, and then decide where to find the information. You may decide that some pieces of information need to be found on the Internet, while you are more likely to look for other types of information in books.

Arrange your ideas on paper before you begin to write up a presentation.

You may find you need to research some information in your school library.

Break It Down

Split the writing into different sections and put them in order, starting with an introduction. Also think about what kind of presentation you will do. Will you use a computer to complete it or will you put it together by hand?

RESEARCHING ON THE INTERNET

TIPS FOR SUCCESS

The Internet contains a huge amount of information, but beware! Many websites are unreliable. You need to check information and rewrite it in your own words. Follow these tips:

- Use websites that belong to organizations you can trust to be accurate. Choose websites that end with .org, for example, rather than .com.

- Be aware of forums and websites that offer opinions rather than facts.

- Do not copy and paste text you have found on the Internet. This is called plagiarism.

PLANNING FOR TESTS

Have you already had to prepare for and take some tests at school? Does your teacher ever give quizzes in class? As you get older, you will take more tests and exams. Don't worry! Good planning will help you do your best.

Preparing for a Test

The best way to prepare for a written test is to review what you are expected to know. Make sure you remember the facts you have been taught. If it is a math test, for example, review and practice the different kinds of problems you are likely to be given. If it is a spelling test, practice your spellings beforehand until you know them inside out. If you have a music test, be sure to rehearse well ahead of time so you are confident on the day.

You are more likely to do well on a test if you plan and prepare for it.

18

Prepare for your music tests by practicing the test piece until you can play it with confidence.

DURING THE TEST

You've done the preparation, and now it's time for the test. What can you do to give yourself the best chance of doing well? Most important of all is to stay calm. Here are some other tips to follow:

- **Breathe deeply:** Before you begin, take some deep breaths and focus on what you are about to do.

- **Read the question:** Begin by reading the question carefully before you start to answer it.

- **Understand the question:** Be sure you understand what is being asked of you.

19

PLAN YOUR LIFE

Do you have money of your own, such as a weekly allowance, which you decide how you spend? Can you earn extra money by doing chores around the house? As you get older, you will be responsible for more money, so getting used to managing your money now will help you later in your life.

Spending and Saving

Do you spend most of your money on snacks and sodas, or are you saving up for a cell phone, tablet, or something else you really want? If you're used to spending all your money, how about saving some of it? After a while, you will have saved a larger amount to spend on other things.

If you are already saving, check that your plan will work. For example, if you are saving $1 a week, how long will it take to save the amount you need?

Earning money for doing extra chores can help you save for something you really want.

Small amounts
of money saved
regularly soon
build into a
larger amount.
Try it out!

PLANNING A BUDGET

TIPS FOR SUCCESS

A budget will help you decide how to use the money that you regularly receive. Here are some basic steps to help you learn to budget:

- Write down how much money you receive every week.
- Make a list of the things you have to buy and how much they cost. For example, you may pay for bus fares.
- Figure out how much that leaves you to spend every week.
- Divide this amount among extra things you want to buy or save for. For instance, you may buy small items but save for larger items that cost more money to buy.

PLANNING A PARTY

There is a lot to plan before you have a party. First, think about what kind of party you are having. Is it a birthday party, a Halloween party, or an outing with your friends? The main objective is to make sure that everyone has a good time—but how will you achieve that?

What You Need to Plan

The main elements of a party are invitations, food, and games or activities. You need to plan all these parts of your party well ahead of time, and before you send out the invitations. Discuss everything with your parents as you go along. Before you can send out invitations, you need to know when and where you will have the party.

You can plan to have your party at a favorite theme park or another venue you like to visit.

Your Party Theme

Next, think about what you will do at the party. You could include a treasure hunt or a visit to the movies. A Halloween party will include costumes, bobbing for apples, and maybe going trick-or-treating. What kind of food will you have? Maybe the whole party is a visit to a favorite restaurant or a visit to a swimming pool you like to go to.

TIPS FOR SUCCESS

MAKING THE INVITATIONS

You can buy packs of invitations on which you only have to fill in the details, but it is fun to make your own. These are the things you need to include:

- Name of the person you're inviting.
- What kind of party you are having.
- The date and time of your party.
- The address or place where the party will be.
- Your name, so everyone knows it is your party!

There is lots to make and do before a Halloween party!

FUNDRAISING FOR CHARITY

Do you have a favorite charity that you like to support? Perhaps you want to help protect endangered animals or support a local charity. Maybe you could organize an event to raise money for it. Think of something fun so that lots of people join in. Make sure you publicize your event so everyone knows about it.

Hold a Sale

One of the easiest ways to raise money is to hold a sale, either at school or a garage or yard sale at home. (Make sure you get permission first!) You could ask people to make cakes and cookies for a bake sale, or ask them to bring items such as toys, books, or DVDs to sell. You could ask your friends and family to help you sell the items, too.

Having a bake sale is a great way to earn extra money.

BAKE SALE TODAY!

Sponsored Event

You could organize a challenge, such as running as many times as possible around the park or a sponsored car wash event in which you wash as many cars as you can. You then ask people to sponsor you a certain amount for every circuit of the park you run or every car you wash. Sponsored events are a great way to raise money and have lots of fun at the same time!

You and your friends could ask people to sponsor you to take part in a running race.

TIPS FOR SUCCESS

COLLECTING THE MONEY

Collecting the money is the most important part of the event!

- If you are having a sale, have a bag or cash box for keeping the money safe.
- After a sponsored event, you need to collect the money that's been pledged. First, get everyone to figure out what people owe them based on what they achieved.
- Tell everyone involved the grand total!

PLANNING FOR A VACATION

What are you going to do during summer vacation? Are there summer school classes or day camps you could go to? Local community or arts centers, sports centers, and schools often run day camps and organized activities. Sleepaway summer camps may last several weeks. They are a good way to make friends.

Getting Ready to Go

There are two main stages to planning for summer camp. First, you and your parents choose the camp and reserve your place. Then, you figure out how to get there. Can you walk or take a bus, or do you need to go by car? The first step is to plan your journey. Closer to the time you leave, you can plan other details, such as what to take with you.

You could use the Internet to help your family plan a trip or vacation.

Summer camps are a good place to try new activities.

Family Vacation

If your whole family is taking a vacation together, your parents will make all the arrangements. You can learn a lot by taking an interest in the plans they make. What do they have to do before you all leave? How does this help you with your own planning?

PACKING YOUR THINGS

TIPS FOR SUCCESS

How do you make sure that you pack everything you need but don't take too much? The answer is to make a list. It might include:

- Change of clothes.
- Swimsuit.
- Towel.
- Sleeping clothes.
- Toiletry bag with toothbrush, toothpaste, soap, washcloth, and so on.
- Hairbrush or comb.
- Sunscreen.
- Book or computer game.

PLAN AHEAD!

Planning skills will help you in middle school, high school, and at college. As you get older, you will have more things to deal with. Planning will help you take control and keep on top of things. Planning involves thinking ahead, and it will soon become automatic. Get a head start now by learning how things happen and how to plan for them.

Going Places

As you get older, you will have to find your own way around. Practice now! If you are on a long car trip, follow the route on a map. Estimate how long the trip will take. If you are flying by plane, notice all the procedures you go through from check-in or dropping off bags to getting to the correct departure gate on time.

> If you are used to planning, you'll be able to plan trips, such as vacations with your friends, when you are older.

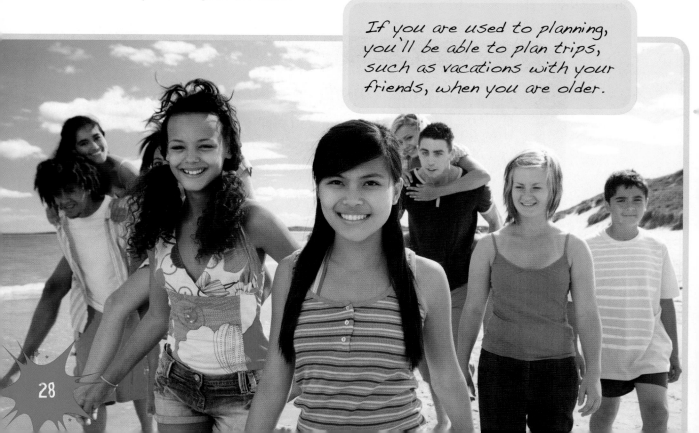

Find out as much as you can about where you are going before you leave for your destination.

Plan for Destinations

If you are going on an outing with your family, find out all you can about where you are going. What type of place are you going to? What will you need to take with you? How should you dress? Then you will know what you want to do when you get there, and how much time you will need to allow for your journey. If you start planning now, you'll be an expert planner when you are older!

TIPS FOR SUCCESS

THINK OF EVERYTHING!

Suppose you are planning an outing for the family. Here are some things to consider:

- **The total cost:** Is the trip affordable?
- **Traveling:** What is the best way to get there?
- **Distance:** How long will the trip take?
- **Check times:** Check the opening and closing times.
- **Eating out:** Will you take food with you or buy it there?

GLOSSARY

automatic doing something so often you do it without thinking

budget a plan for estimating how money received will be used and spent

charity an organization that collects money, which it spends to help people, animals, and other good causes

check-in a desk run by an airline at an airport where passengers confirm that they have arrived for a journey

checklist a list of things to be done or remembered

deadline a date or time at which something must be done by

departure gate the door or passageway through which passengers leave the airport building to reach their airplane

endangered animals animals that are in danger of becoming extinct—that is, of dying out altogether

focusing concentrating

forums Internet message boards

hazards risks

objective what is aimed for

outcome what results from an action or actions

plagiarism copying and using someone else's words and passing them off as your own

presentation communication and explanation of information or ideas

publicize to make something known to many people

recharge to refill with energy or power

research to find out facts and information or to test ideas

review to go over information already learned

routine a fixed way of doing things

sidetracked diverted or moved away from the correct course

sponsored given money in support of a cause

FOR MORE INFORMATION

BOOKS

Espeland, Pamela, and Elizabeth Verdick. *See You Later, Procrastinator! (Get It Done)*. Laugh & Learn. Minneapolis, MN: Free Spirit Publishing, 2008.

Romain, Trevor. *How to Do Homework Without Throwing Up*. Laugh & Learn. Minneapolis, MN: Free Spirit Publishing, 2005.

Somerville, Barbara A. *Studying and Tests*. Chicago, IL: Heinemann Library, 2009.

WEBSITES

This website for kids gives you good advice on how to manage your allowance. It includes comments posted by kids.
www.cyh.com/HealthTopics/HealthTopicDetailsKids.
aspx?p=335&np=282&id=2235

This website about planning homework is written for teenagers, but you can find some useful tips here to help you now as well as later.
kidshealth.org/teen/school_jobs/school/homework.html

This website about how to plan a party is written for parents, but it has lots of advice and information that you can use, too.
www.kidspartyfun.com/pages/planningguide.html

INDEX